This is for every brave researcher, for all the intelligent scientists, and for our wonderful planet.

Mario Cuesta Hernando

This is for my brave friend, Flor. While I was drawing these pictures, she was on the most dangerous sea voyage imaginable.

Raquel Martín

Library of Congress Control Number: 2020933398
A CIP catalogue record for this book is available from the British Library.

Translation: Paul Kelly
Project management: Melanie Schöni
Copyediting: John Son
Production management and typesetting: Susanne Hermann

Prestel Publishing compensates the CO_2 emissions produced from the making of this book by supporting a reforestation project in Brazil. Find further information on the project here: www.ClimatePartner.com/14044-1912-1001

Penguin Random House Verlagsgruppe FSC® N001967

Printed in Italy

ISBN 978-3-7913-7456-7
www.prestel.com

ANTARCTICA

A Continent of Wonder

MARIO CUESTA HERNANDO
RAQUEL MARTÍN

PRESTEL

Munich · London · New York

Things You Will Discover in This Book

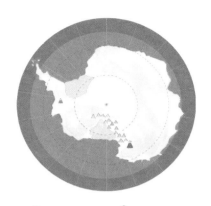

Penguins

What Is Being Researched in Antarctica?

Seals

Beware, Snowstorm!

A Home in the Ice

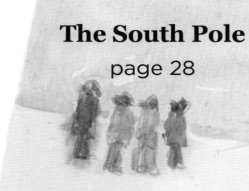

The South Pole

Dangers to Antarctica

Volcanoes: Fire and Ice

The Hard Winter

Antarctica

—

A Continent of Wonder

What luck! The United States Antarctic Program has invited me on an expedition to the Antarctic. Together with scientists from all over the world, I will spend the summertime in the Southern Hemisphere from November to April. We are sailing together on the *Polar Star,* an oceanographic research vessel, and we will visit the McMurdo Station, a research station in the south of the continent next to the Ross Sea.

Antarctica is a truly record-breaking continent. The lowest temperatures (-128.6° F / -89.2° C) and the strongest hurricanes (199 mph / 327 km/h) on earth have been measured here. The ice can be up to 2.5 miles (4 km) thick! And 67 percent of the world's freshwater reserves are in the Antarctic—frozen solid.

I am so excited about this trip! But before we leave, can we just get something clear once and for all? Penguins live in Antarctica, polar bears do not. And there are polar bears in the Arctic, but no penguins.

Let's get started!

I take my diary on the journey.

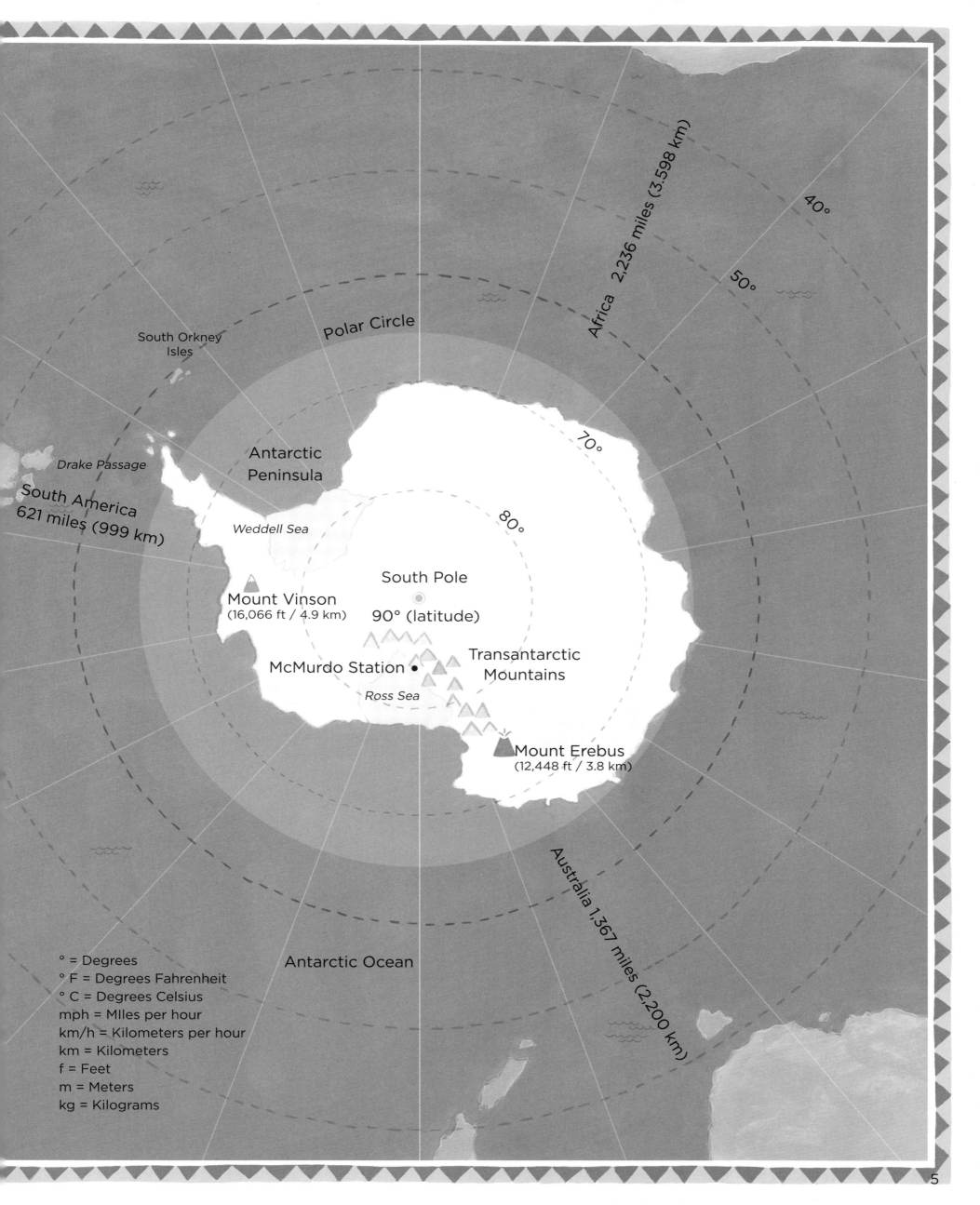

Africa 2.236 miles (3.598 km)

40°

50°

South Orkney
Isles

Polar Circle

70°

Drake Passage

Antarctic
Peninsula

South America
621 miles (999 km)

Weddell Sea

80°

South Pole

Mount Vinson
(16,066 ft / 4.9 km)

90° (latitude)

McMurdo Station •

Transantarctic
Mountains

Ross Sea

Mount Erebus
(12,448 ft / 3.8 km)

Australia 1,367 miles (2.200 km)

Antarctic Ocean

° = Degrees
° F = Degrees Fahrenheit
° C = Degrees Celsius
mph = MIles per hour
km/h = Kilometers per hour
km = Kilometers
f = Feet
m = Meters
kg = Kilograms

With a wingspan of almost 10 feet (3.33 m), the wandering albatross has the largest wings in the bird kingdom. Throughout the whole year, it is either in flight or floating on the ocean's surface. Thunderstorms like this one barely cause harm to the albatross.

Journey through the Drake Passage

Between Cape Horn, the southernmost tip of South America, and Antarctica stretches the wildest sea in the world, the dreaded Drake Passage. Ships like ours have to cope with waves up to 23 feet high (7 m), as well as fierce storms. In the past, sailors who had managed to get around Cape Horn used to wear an earring on their left ear as a sign of their courage. Ahoy and let's go Captain, no fear and full steam ahead!

Cape Horn

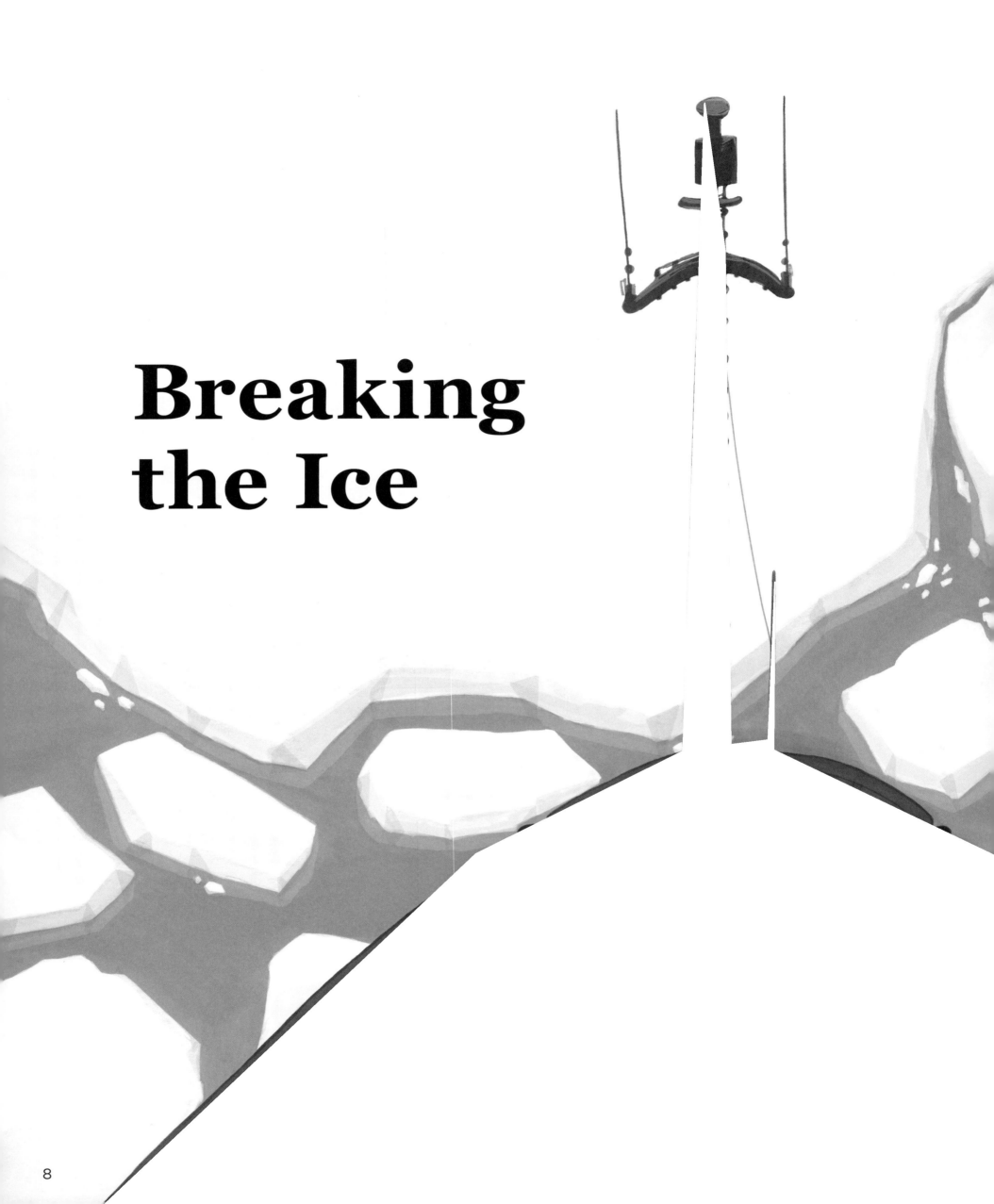

Breaking
the Ice

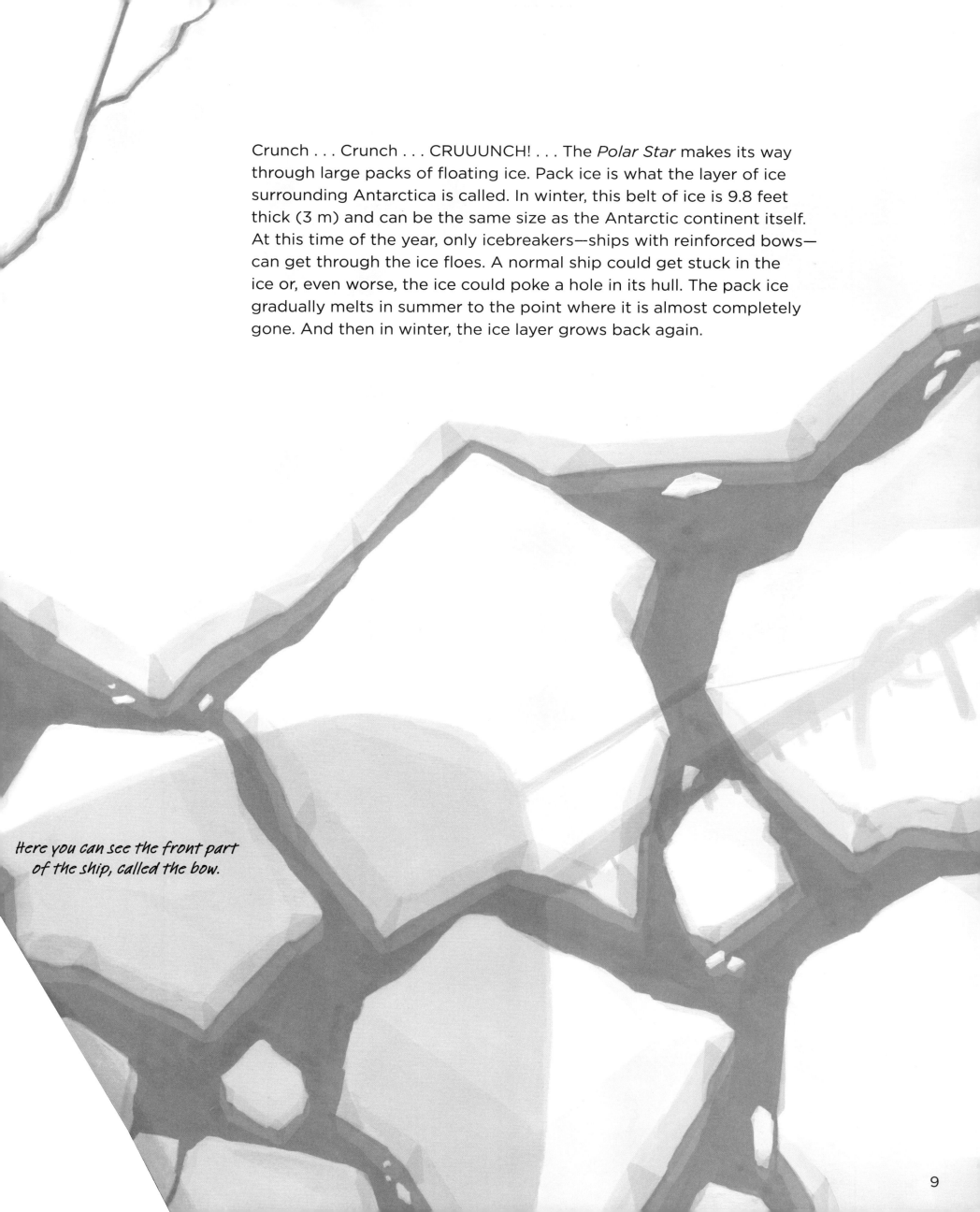

Crunch . . . Crunch . . . CRUUUNCH! . . . The *Polar Star* makes its way through large packs of floating ice. Pack ice is what the layer of ice surrounding Antarctica is called. In winter, this belt of ice is 9.8 feet thick (3 m) and can be the same size as the Antarctic continent itself. At this time of the year, only icebreakers—ships with reinforced bows—can get through the ice floes. A normal ship could get stuck in the ice or, even worse, the ice could poke a hole in its hull. The pack ice gradually melts in summer to the point where it is almost completely gone. And then in winter, the ice layer grows back again.

Here you can see the front part of the ship, called the bow.

We Arrive in Antarctica

Kelp Gull

Finally, we are at the Antarctic itself. After several days at sea, we have reached the continent. The ice is piling up into giant walls and there are icebergs floating all around us. Only 1 percent of the Antarctic is free of ice. Some icebergs are miles thick and others are tiny. Although it is two in the morning, the sun is already shining. It is only dark in summer for three hours a day.

A humpback whale jumps out of the water to communicate with other whales . . . or maybe it's just having fun.

Exposed ice filters sunlight in such a way that only blue remains. That's why icebergs appear to be blue.

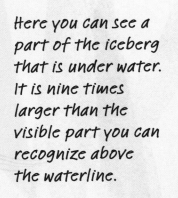

Here you can see a part of the iceberg that is under water. It is nine times larger than the visible part you can recognize above the waterline.

Underwater World

Life teems under the keel of our ship. Though the average water temperature is 28° F (-2° C), the Antarctic Ocean is home to the oldest and most biodiverse ecosystem on earth. Scientists are discovering new species every day. Do you know which creature is the most common in the world? It is krill, which is a tiny shrimp-like crustacean that lives in huge shoals in the sea. Penguins, fish, seals, and whales feed on krill.

These almost-transparent fish are called crocodile icefish. There is a natural antifreeze agent in their cells that prevents them from turning into ice.

Diving robots help research the animal kingdom in the deep.

Krill

This ice stalactite, which is like an underwater icicle, has trapped several starfish on the seafloor that did not get away in time.

Sponges are multicellular animals that live in all seas. The sponges in the Antarctic Ocean are huge and can live up to 10,000 years.

The legs of this sea spider are almost 16 feet (4.8 m) long!

Whales

Several whale species spend their summertime in the Antarctic. We saw each and every one of them on our trip. It was only a few years ago that whales could be hunted without any restrictions. And because of that they almost completely disappeared from the oceans. Thankfully, the population is now recovering.

Humpback Whale
60 feet (18 m)

These whales cover huge distances across all the world's oceans. In the course of a year, they can travel over 15,500 miles (25,000 km). They spend their summers grazing at the earth's poles and their winters swimming toward the equator to reproduce. They are famous for their acrobatic leaps out of the water.

Finback Whale
90 feet (27 m)

The finback is the second biggest member of the whale family and, with a top speed of just over 30 mph (48 km/h), one of the fastest. It lives in small groups out in the open sea.

Blue Whale
109 feet (33 m)

Blue whales are the largest animals that have ever existed on earth. They are even bigger than the dinosaurs and can weigh up to 200 tons (181.4 MT). Their heart alone weighs around 440 pounds (200 kg). Yet, although blue whales are gigantic, they feed on krill, the tiniest of animals, easily polishing off around 6,600 pounds (3,000 kg) a day!

Killer Whale

30 feet (9 m)

You cannot tell by looking at them, but killer whales are actually part of the dolphin family. As a matter of fact, they are the largest dolphins on the planet. These clever and social creatures live and hunt in groups, a little bit like wolves, except at sea. They mainly feed on fish, penguins, and seals.

Sperm Whale

60 feet (18 m)

Sperm whales have the biggest teeth in the animal kingdom. They are also excellent divers. They can remain underwater for over an hour and dive nearly two miles (3.2 km) deep toward the very bottom of the ocean, where they hunt their favorite food—squid.

Here is our diver, Maria. In comparison to her, you can get a good idea of the size of the whales.

Antarctic Minke Whale

33 feet (10 m)

Compared to the rest of the whale family, these whales are quite small. They can be found throughout the waters of the Southern Hemisphere but gather in Antarctica during the summer months. The Arctic minke whale, which is a distant cousin, spends its time in the Northern Hemisphere.

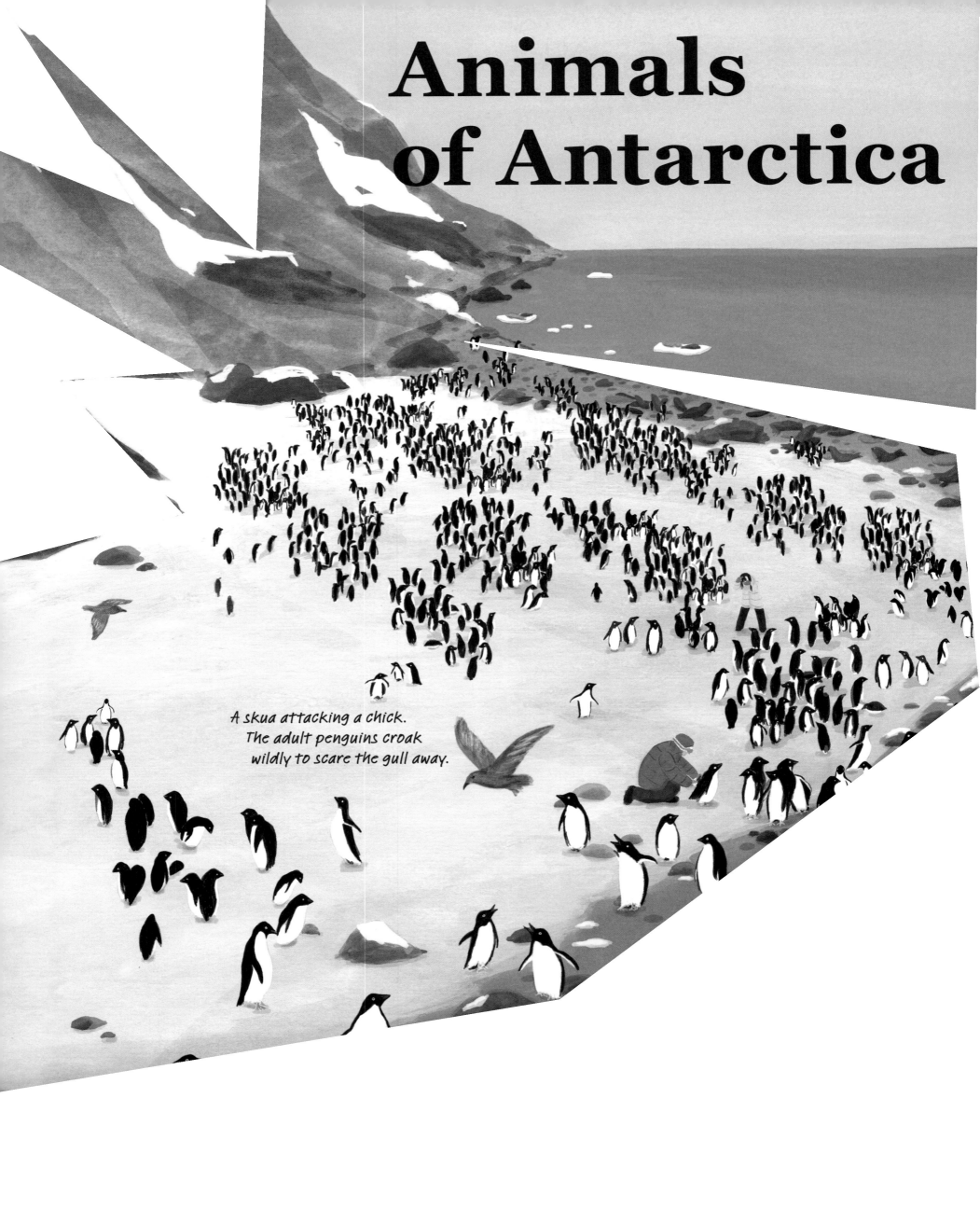

Animals
of Antarctica

A skua attacking a chick.
The adult penguins croak
wildly to scare the gull away.

What an enormous crowd of penguins, seals, sea lions, and elephant seals in one heap! The Adélie penguins that you see here live in giant colonies with up to 180,000 nests. Adélie penguins can spend several days in the water searching for food to feed their chicks. When they are on land, they keep a sharp lookout for great skuas which like to snatch away their eggs and freshly hatched young. Seals, on the other hand, need not worry about anything on land. They can spend the whole long, lovely day thinking about how lucky they are to live in such a place.

Researchers from the McMurdo Station have been involved with these penguins for several years.

Penguins

Penguins are, without a doubt, part of the seabird family, but they are unable to fly. They are, however, excellent swimmers and divers who use their wings like oars in the water. They feed on krill, small fish, and squid. Their plumage and the fat under their skin protect them from the cold. In addition, their blood and bones have evolved in such a way that they are able to dive to great depths for minutes on end.

Gentoo Penguin
35 inches (89 cm)

The gentoo penguin can be easily identified by its red beak and white markings above its eyes. Oh, and by its honking call, which sounds almost like a donkey's. At 22 mph (35 km/h), it is the fastest swimmer of all the penguins. Up until a few years ago, the gentoo only lived on Antarctica's surrounding islands, but due to global warming they have relocated onto the Antarctic Peninsula.

A four-month-old emperor penguin chick with down fluff.

Emperor Penguin
47 inches (119 cm)

Emperor penguins are the largest penguins and the only ones to spend winter in the Antarctic and raise their young there during this time. This species lives in colonies in the region's interior, up to 60 miles (97 km) away from the sea. An emperor penguin can dive as deep as 1,800 feet (550 m) and remain under water for a full twenty minutes!

Macaroni Penguin
28 inches (71 cm)

There are several penguin types that are crested, but only this gold-crested penguin lives in the Antarctic. It sports strikingly long, golden feathers above its eyes. Although macaroni penguins have the largest population of all the penguin species, their numbers are dwindling due to fishing, ocean warming, and pollution.

King Penguin
35 inches (89 cm)

King penguins look a bit like emperor penguins, but they are slightly smaller than their relatives and do not live in the Antarctic but on the surrounding islands.

Chinstrap Penguin
30 inches (76 cm)

Its distinguishing feature is the black stripe above its throat, which gives the species its name. Chinstrap penguins live in enormous colonies of up to a million breeding pairs.

Adélie Penguin
26 inches (66 cm)

The emperor and adélie penguins are the only penguin species that inhabit the whole of the Southern Continent. All the other species live on the Antarctic Peninsula. Adélie penguins build their nests out of rocks. But not with just any old stone. They carefully select each rock and use only the best ones to make their nests.

This is how an Adélie penguin develops: the chick is still covered in down fluff after hatching, but from then onward it begins to grow feathers.

Seals

The scientific name for seals, sea lions, and elephant seals is "pinniped," which means "fin-footed animal." There are several pinnipeds living in Antarctica, but they can also be found elsewhere. In the past, seals have been found living, quite comfortably one would imagine, in the Mediterranean.

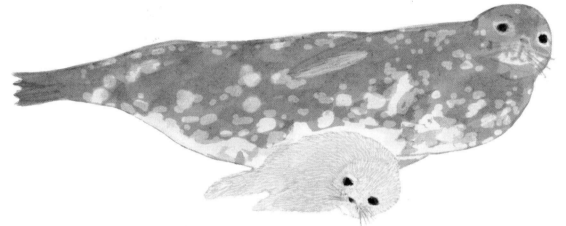

Weddell Seal
10 feet (3 m), 1,200 pounds (544 kg)

There is no other mammal in the southernmost regions of the earth like the Weddell seal. It is the only mammal that spends the winter in Antarctica. And because the water is warmer than the air, it no longer goes ashore but only occasionally pops its head out of the water to breathe.

Weddell seal pup

Leopard Seal
10 feet (3 m), 815 pounds (370 kg)

This is one of the most feared predators of the Antarctic. While other seals just feed on fish, krill, and octopus, sea leopards also eat penguins and even young seals of other species.

Here is a sketch of a leopard seal's skull. Do you see the sharp teeth?

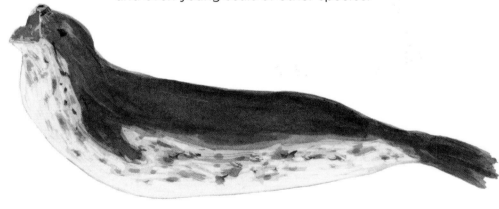

Ross Seal
6.5 feet (2 m), 440 pounds (200 kg)

The smallest, rarest, and least studied of Antarctic pinnipeds, this seal communicates underwater by whistling, which makes for a strange sound.

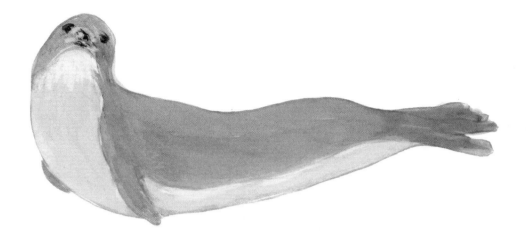

Crabeater Seals
7.5 feet (2.3 m), 440 pounds (200 kg)

This seal owes its name to its special diet. This exceptional type of seal is unique in that it eats krill by swallowing water open-mouthed and then pressing it out through its teeth. This way, the krill gets stuck in its mouth – just like small fish.

Sea Lion
8 feet (2.5 m), 397 pounds (181 kg)

Sea lions are also a member of the seal family, but they differ through their clearly visible ears and their stronger front flippers, which they use to support themselves on land. Like other seals, they feed on a variety of fish and krill.

Southern Elephant Seal
Male: up to 19 feet (5.8 m), 8,800 pounds (4,000 kg)
Female: 9 feet (2.8 m), 1,112–1,472 pounds (600–800 kg)

Elephant seals owe their name to the trunk-shaped nose of the male. During the breeding season, these males can often be seen fighting on the beach.

The two male Elephant seals fight for their territory and the favor of the females.

What Is Being Researched in Antarctica?

Climate researchers use this giant balloon to study the atmosphere.

Millions of years ago, there used to be many plants and animals in the Antarctic.

That is why paleontologists look for fossils in the rocks, to learn about plant and animals that have become extinct.

The next months at the station are entirely devoted to science. The researchers here come from all parts of the world. In Antarctica, all states support each other and use their research stations and their ships together. Since humans have never settled here and the environment has not been polluted, there is no better place to explore the earth. It could be said that Antarctica is a gigantic natural laboratory.

The glacier is slowly edging toward the sea little by little. Glacier researchers, called glaciologists, use rods to measure the movement of the ice and glaciers.

Ice samples are taken from the glacier using a drill. This ice was created thousands of years ago. And it still contains clues as to what the earth was like back then.

Beware, Snowstorm!

The wind in Antarctica is almost as dangerous as the cold. Winds can reach up to 190 mph (305 km/h). Not surprisingly, Antarctica is the windiest place on earth. The wind can whirl up so much snow from the ground that you cannot see your hand in front of your face. It is far too dangerous to stay outside in this weather, which means the researchers have to stay inside the station. They also make sure their instruments and kits are secure so that they are not damaged by the fierce winds. It sometimes takes days for the weather to become calm enough for the researchers to safely leave their stations.

The research station is only fully manned during the Southern Hemisphere's summer, which lasts from November to April. In the winter, only a small team remains on the site. As much research work as possible is carried out during these summer months.

Some penguins become completely snowed in. Thankfully, they are well equipped to withstand the cold.

A Home in the Ice

It is hard to believe how warm it is inside the station while the icy winds rage outside. Until the storm has eased off, the scientists prepare for their next investigations, read books and texts about their field of research, as well as exchange ideas and relax.

This researcher is speaking with her family in the US by video conference.

When the weather is nice enough, everyone stays outside the whole day. Electricity at the station is generated by solar panels and wind turbines, and all waste is recycled. The researchers strive to leave the smallest possible carbon footprint in Antarctica.

The runway
where you arrive
by plane.

The Ceremonial South Pole is a metallic sphere
on top of a short barber pole located at latitude
90 degrees south. It is surrounded by the flags of the
countries that have signed the Antarctic Treaty.

The South Pole

Around our earth is the equator, a belt that divides the earth into southern
and northern hemispheres. The equator is at 0° and the Arctic North Pole at
the top of Earth is at +90°. At the opposite end of the planet, the Antarctic
South Pole is at -90°. This information helps us determine where in the world
we are. No matter which direction you look here, you are always looking to
the north. There is no west or east. We are almost at the center of Antarctica.
The ice extends for hundreds of miles around us and is nearly two miles
deep below us. The United States runs a large research station here, which
is also active in the winter. In honor of the first two major expeditions to
the South Pole, it is called the Amundsen–Scott South Pole Station.

28

In 1911, the Norwegian Roald Amundsen and the Briton Robert Scott raced each other to be the first humans to reach the South Pole. Amundsen won, but Scott made some very significant scientific discoveries.

Roald Amundsen

Robert Falcon Scott

For example, Scott found this fossil of a tree. This and other finds have shown that the continents were connected to each other millions of years ago.

Photo of Amundsen and his team arriving at the South Pole.

You can observe very distant stars with this telescope. And because there is no air pollution in Antarctica, no light generated by tall houses, and because we are very high up, this observatory is regarded as one of the best in the world.

South Pole Telescope (SPT)

Volcanoes: Fire and Ice

Fire in the middle of the ice? What is that all about? There are some fairly large mountains in the Antarctic, some of which can reach over 13,000 feet (3.9 km). The highest one on the continent is in fact Mount Vinson at 16,066 feet (4.9 km). Here you can see Mount Erebus (12,448 ft / 3.8 km). There are fewer than ten open lava lakes all over the world. This is one of them. The hot gases of the volcano melt snow and ice, creating tunnels and smokestacks.

The Transantarctic Mountains stretch over a distance of 2,174 miles (3,500 km).

Ice Oven

This tunnel is hundreds of feet deep. To research it, scientists climb down by holding onto a rope.

The heat of
the liquid lava
is 1.832° F (1,000° C)!

...entists
examine
the volcanic
crater.

Dangers to Antarctica

A couple of tourists are no problem, but mass tourism poses a great threat to Antarctica.

What a pity! It is already time to say goodbye to Antarctica. After an impressive month, we travel home. The researchers go back on board the *Polar Star* and only the winter team remains at McMurdo Station.

As beautiful as Antarctica is, it is in great danger due to the actions of humans. Under no circumstances should we allow this continent to be destroyed.

Lurking Dangers

· Global warming
· Climate change
· Melting ice
· Overfishing
· Mass tourism
· Non-native species
· Mining and oil production
· Pollution

Invasive populations are another problem. When seeds are accidentally brought to Antarctica on the soles of shoes worn by scientists and tourists, for example, they can grow uncontrolled and displace local species.

Some ships catch more fish than they are permitted to, others fish protected species.

The Hard Winter

Winter has begun. It is now nighttime twenty-four hours a day. Yes, you read that right! The sun no longer rises and the cold becomes unbearable. It can get down to -58° F (-50° C)! In these conditions, only a few research stations are in operation. Even the majority of animals have migrated north, away from Antarctica. Only the male emperor penguins stay behind to keep their eggs safe and warm while the females are off

The polar lights at the South Pole are called "aurora australis". These fascinating light spectacles appear in winter when electrically charged particles from the sun meet gas particles in the air.

In order to keep each other warm, the emperor penguins cuddle up tight to each other. Otherwise, they would freeze.

filling their bellies until the end of winter, when they return to feed the chicks. The males really have to endure very extreme conditions, but at least they can marvel at the colorful spectacle of the southern lights.

35

The Antarctic Treaty

Antarctica is the planet's loneliest continent. The region is one and a half times the size of Europe or the United States, but it does not actually belong to anyone. No country can lay claim to it, meaning Antarctica belongs to all of us.

The climate is so harsh that people have never settled here. When Antarctica was discovered, some countries wanted to secure a part of it for themselves. However, since several countries wanted to own the same region, an agreement could not be reached. It almost came to war until, finally, the Antarctic Treaty was signed in Washington in 1959.

This agreement is the only one that applies in the Antarctic. It is an international law and relates to the whole world.

The Antarctic Treaty states:

· Antarctica does not currently belong to anyone. It is there for all humanity.

· Every country that accepts the Antarctic Treaty is permitted to carry out research there.

· Antarctica is a continent of peace. Military activities and atomic weapons tests are forbidden.

· The continent is reserved for science. Scientists are privileged.

· Individual states are obliged to cooperate. They are duty-bound to accommodate scientists from other countries in their own research stations and ships.

· Nature must be preserved at all costs.

· Any pollution or leaving of waste is strictly prohibited.

· Mining and oil production is prohibited.

· Fishing is limited.

Who Discovered Antarctica?

For hundreds of years, geographers drew a continent called Terra Australis Incognita (Latin for "unknown country in the south") at the place where Antarctica can be seen on a world map today. It was a place no human eyes had yet seen.

Even the Ancient Greeks suspected that a huge continent had to exist in the south to act as a counterbalance to the known land masses in the Northern Hemisphere. It was a long time, however, until it was discovered.

In 1603, the Spanish navigator and explorer, Gabriel de Castilla, got caught up in a storm as he was sailing around Cape Horn. The wind drove his ship far south. On his return, he reported seeing snow-capped mountains, which could possibly have been Antarctica, but that is not certain.

Two hundred years later, in 1819, the British seal hunter, William Smith, got caught in a storm and drifted down to the Antarctic Peninsula. He is now seen as the first person to have set eyes on the continent.

After him, a great many Antarctic explorers ploughed through the ice right up until 1914. Bellinghausen, Weddell, d'Urville, Wilkes, Ross, de Gerlache, Scott, Drygalski, Nordenskjöld, Charcot, Shackleton, Shirase, Amundsen, and Mawson all traveled bravely southward and made important contributions to science.

Since then, Antarctica has been and continues to be researched by countless scientists from all over the world. There are too many for them all to be listed, even if their work is as important as that of the earlier pioneers and that of all future Antarctic expeditions. If reading this book has made you eager to travel to Antarctica, you may as well become a scientist yourself and set off to discover more secrets of this wonderful continent.

Things to Know about Antarctica

United States Antarctic Program (USAP): is an organization of the US government which has a presence in Antarctica. It was founded in 1959 and manages all US scientific research and related logistics in Antarctica as well as aboard ships in the Southern Ocean.

Antarctic Ice Sheet: The Antarctic ice sheet is made up of all the glaciers in the region and, at 5.4 million square miles (13.9 million sq km), forms the largest ice mass on earth.

Antarctic Peninsula: If you look at Antarctica on a map, you will see an arm on the left that stretches out toward South America. This is the Antarctic Peninsula. And the rest of the continent is divided into West Antarctica (below the Peninsula) and East Antarctica.

Antarctic (Polar) Circle: This is located at 66 degrees latitude south. During the summer months, you can see the sun for twenty-four hours, even at midnight when it is called the midnight sun. In the winter months, you can witness the polar night, when the night lasts for more than twenty-four hours. At the South Pole, which is the southernmost point on earth, the polar day and polar night each last six months. The same thing happens at the North Pole in the Arctic Circle.

Antarctic Circumpolar Current: This is a cold ocean current flowing west to east around the Antarctic. Because it is not stopped by any landmass the current is very strong.

Heroic Age of Antarctic Exploration: From the end of the nineteenth century right through to the 1920s, numerous adventurers set off to explore Antarctica. They all had to endure enormous hardships and some even perished.

Latitude: This is the distance north or south of the equator measured in degrees. The equator is 0 degrees and the South Pole is 90 degrees south, while the North Pole is at 90 degrees north. Every latitude in between represents a line around the earth that runs parallel to the equator.

60 Degrees South: The Antarctic Treaty applies to all areas south of this point, including all ice shelves and islands.

Iceberg: Gigantic tabletop icebergs are typical for Antarctica, breaking away from glaciers and then drifting thousands of miles in the sea.

Glacier: This is a giant icefield that forms from old snow masses on land. Icefields formed on the sea are known as pack ice.

Hemisphere: The earth is divided into two halves, which are known as the Northern and Southern Hemispheres. The line between the two hemispheres on the center of the globe is called the equator.

International Polar Year: Many different countries organize scientific activities to further research the poles in this special year. Since 1882, the International Polar Year has been taking place every fifty years, with the last one occurring in 2007–2008.

Cooperation: This simply means working together, which is really important in Antarctica. Every country, scientist, naval captain, and all other visitors to the Antarctic must truly cooperate with each other in order to thrive in such a hostile environment. Actually, this should apply to the entire world.

Marine Research Vessel: A floating laboratory specially equipped for the ocean.

McMurdo Station: This is one of three US Antarctic science facilities. It is located on the south tip of Ross Island in the very south of the continent. This station is the largest community in Antarctica and is capable of housing around 1,200 residents in the summer. *Polar Star* is the only ship in the United States' fleet large enough to break the heavy sea ice to access McMurdo.

Ecosystem: This is how we describe the community of all living creatures in a certain habitat. It includes the living space itself and especially the relationships between living things with each other and with their living space.

Protocol on Environmental Protection to the Antarctic Treaty: Agreed upon in Madrid in 1991, this treaty commits us to protecting the Antarctic environment—the number one priority on the continent. Which is why mining and oil production are banned in Antarctica.

The Antarctic and Climate Change

When we talk about climate change nowadays, we mean the global warming of our planet caused by humans. By burning oil, coal, and gas to generate energy for cars, factories, computers, or cell phones, we are creating greenhouse gases. One of them is carbon dioxide (CO_2). This gas makes the protective shell surrounding our earth— the atmosphere—increasingly dense. Heat builds up beneath just like in a greenhouse for plants. This is why our planet has gradually been getting hotter and hotter.

Since Antarctica is one of the places on earth where climate change is happening the fastest, scientists can study the effects of climate change especially well here.

Global warming is causing the ice to melt in Antarctica. The huge glaciers are shrinking year by year. When these large masses of ice melt, their water flows into the Southern Ocean, which cause the sea levels of all oceans to rise. This is dangerous because many humans and animals live by the sea. If sea levels continue to rise, islands and coastal locations around the world, such as Venice (Italy) and Miami (Florida) will soon be under water

This melting of the ice also affects those animals living in Antarctica. Penguins that usually live on the ice now have to migrate to other locations.

Both the Antarctic and Arctic Circles are at risk. Together, we have to make sure these wonderful and extremely important regions have the chance of a future. If we humans change our lifestyle by using fewer fossil fuels by driving and flying less and reducing our carbon footprint by recycling more and eating less meat, we can help protect our world and all its living beings.